The Forest of
Sure Things

Tupelo Press/*Crazyhorse* Book Award
Previously the Tupelo Press First Book Award

Published with the generous support of

home of the journal *Crazyhorse*.

Jennifer Michael Hecht, *The Last Ancient World*
Selected by Janet Holmes

Aimee Nezhukumatathil, *Miracle Fruit*
Selected by Gregory Orr

Bill Van Every, *Devoted Creatures*
Selected by Thomas Lux

David Petruzelli, *Everyone Coming Toward You*
Selected by Campbell McGrath

Lillias Bever, *Bellini in Istanbul*
Selected by Michael Collier

Dwaine Rieves, *When the Eye Forms*
Selected by Carolyn Forché

Kristin Bock, *Cloisters*
Selected by David St. John

Jennifer Militello, *Flinch of Song*
Megan Snyder-Camp, *The Forest of Sure Things*
Selected by Carol Ann Davis, Garrett Doherty, and Jeffrey Levine

The Forest of
Sure Things

Poems by Megan Snyder-Camp

2/11

*To Deborah,
with many thanks, in
this wonderful place.*

Megan Snyder-Camp

TUPELO PRESS
North Adams, Massachusetts

The Forest of Sure Things

Copyright 2010 Megan Snyder-Camp. All rights reserved.

Library of Congress Cataloging-in-Publication Data

Snyder-Camp, Megan.
The forest of sure things : poems / Megan Snyder-Camp. -- 1st paperback ed.
    p. cm. -- (Tupelo press/Crazyhorse book award)
 ISBN 978-1-932195-88-0 (pbk. : alk. paper)
I. Title.
PS3619.N96F67 2010
 811'.6--dc22

2010019950

COVER AND TEXT DESIGNED BY HOWARD KLEIN.

First paperback edition: August 2010.
14 13 12 11 10   5 4 3 2 1

Printed in the United States.

Cover art: "Hive Paths" by Amy Casey (www.amycaseypainting.com). Acrylic painting on paper, 2007. Private collection. Image courtesy of Zg Gallery, Inc., 300 West Superior Street, Chicago, Illinois 60654, www.ZgGallery.com

Epigraphs: Quotation from Alice Munro is from "The Bear Came Over the Mountain," in the book *Hateship, Friendship, Courtship, Loveship, Marriage: Stories* (Vintage, 2002). The quotation from Diane Arbus is from "Five Photographs from Diane Arbus" in *Artforum* (May 1971), cited in the book *Revelations* (Random House, 2003).

Tupelo Press
P.O. Box 1767, North Adams, Massachusetts 01247
Telephone: (413) 664–9611 / Fax: (413) 664–9711
editor@tupelopress.org / www.tupelopress.org

Tupelo Press is an award-winning independent literary press that publishes fine fiction, non-fiction, and poetry in books that are a joy to hold as well as read. Tupelo Press is a registered 501(c)3 non-profit organization, and we rely on public support to carry out our mission of publishing extraordinary work that may be outside the realm of large commercial publishers. Financial donations are welcome and are tax deductible.

NATIONAL
ENDOWMENT
FOR THE ARTS

Supported in part by an award from the National Endowment for the Arts *for Henry and Calliope*

Contents

Two

ONE

Sea Creatures of the Deep

O sockeye O rock sole O starry flounder
O red Irish lord O spiny lumpsucker

Dear threespine stickleback, sweet broken-backed shrimp—
hear the dreadful voices from the balcony. You're the blind

taking the bull by the horns. You're snow on a stick,
a stuck jukebox, a ribbon-swamped trike. O gum boot,

O lemon peel nudibranch—do not fear the leafy horn-mouth;
dogwinkle and moon snail walk the floor and burn their bridges.

Lonely whitecap limpet, days are not true. You stand on one foot,
and we brush past. To live a life is not to walk across a field.

Pity the ghost shrimp, heart on his sleeve, or the glassy sea squirt,
run through with tears. O to have gathered no moss, to know a clam's

muddy joy. You shut with a snap, you blur with silt, you poke
among barnacles. A bunch of one-trick ponies, even brave wolf-eel.

Cornered, the plainfin midshipman sings when afraid.
They say it fears only the elusive cloud sponge.

Borrowed Memory

There ought to be one place you thought about and knew about
and maybe longed for—but never did get to see.

—ALICE MUNRO

The House on Laurel Hill Lane

Between the neighbor's cherry trees
a hat wove through spokes of fruit.
Small birds unshook from the pages of trees.

She went in, laid out plates and glasses, let old news
foam the room. At midnight the phone would ring
only to click aside. How about a sandwich,

he would say, how about some milk.
These miles of threaded oyster beds,
of just-for-show chimneys. How about
these tinted windows? How when the shore
skirted pails, hollows, then stranded razor clams one by one?

They ate well. Even as the words
shifted on her tongue, as the new pitch
caught hold inside her,
as sand rounded out the garage.

She knew when love unwound her but not how.
Let your hair down over the briar patch,
she read to her daughter from the little golden book,
the two tales sewing each other up.

Bearings

The marriage ran under their skin, a rash, or maybe
all that red wine, luminescent cocktail hours
in which lost books were rediscovered, or just a rash,
a reaction sending out runners across her chest,
a vine, something close, ruby scarves coming back
into fashion, their son coming back
from school, from the yard, but now, dinnertime
and the family parted, split houses, her ex and his anger
spread down the long hallway of their house
and into the windows of her new apartment, their daughter's doubled
beds, her doubled face in family portraits that double
in frequency, a family set down and another, this dinnertime
and more red wine, our faces flush with love and sympathy,
the mother decides to see the son again, and so
our doubled flashlights giving us heaven and earth,
all of it safe or at least unmoving, the tall fence
her ex built to hide the little grave, to guard the lot
in this registered historic district (all of the houses
bear their stories on a plaque, their first stories,
run-on, this little town with no street lights, just moon,
cedars), the tall fence behind which is the yard, blue,
in this yard no marker stone and under this stone
their son's everything, no double,
no double

Our Shipwrecks Build Houses

Each creature emerges from a thicket
in this pop-up book, slowly
so you can see it. An owl
using our headlights to track a kill
on the way home from last night's dinner,
a wreck of sauces and painters
in the art critic's cabin by the bay, her talk of paint,
pain, the tides, streaks of red reflected onto our plates,
her two husbands who'd both slowly died,
how over dessert I'd said
it must've seemed the room was emptying
and she'd said no, it was never empty, and I'd said louder
emptying, those men dying
beyond me, your dinner guest—

I barely knew you. Another story that night
I took for my novel: a local girl
the town's first birth in a century.
Her brother stillborn. Years—even now—
I made a home of their loss, adjusted their beds,
added a third child, erased her.
          But that night at least
I left you, your new wood stove, your painters
who'd peaked just before the Berlin Wall fell, not after,

nothing after … the drive home
past boxy statues in the park, heralds
of unmentioned sickness: what does anyone do
with such quiet, what plaque answers it—

***

This week Fort Clatsop has burned,
not the original but the second replica:

bicentennial committee helpless
as the houses' houses are doused and gone.

***

Our turn, our street:
here at her mailbox a pink-haired girl, the first
in a hundred years. Her friends
have not been born yet. Above her
a hummingbird pivots, unsure.
Inside the girl a field of reeds, a year of hinges,
her father's boat crossing the wide water.
She calls her cat in,
Bu-ddy. Bud-dy. Calls
until someone calls her back.

***

No mail today.
The road to Oysterville curves left
until it becomes the road from Oysterville,
easy, the birds in their sanctuary
unaware you've arrived.
Say you brought seed for them,
a tape recorder for the frogs.
Say your telescope won't work.
You could be here all day
and still your father would ask
the same thing he always asks.
One birth doesn't mend another.
The cranberries float in their beds, seasick.

***

Our shipwrecks build houses.
A map of wrecks marks the center
of town, with photos of early log cabins
on this sandy spit of land.
It takes a certain forgetfulness
to see lumber in aftermath.
No wonder no one here
remembers their dreams.
Headlines tell what washed up,
not what went wrong but what
we have here.

***

Once a pair of aviator's goggles,
once hundreds of oranges, whole.
I was not the one born here
but you taught me
how to skim the floor,
how not to skip your records:
you could buy a new one every day
and I'd know it by the silence
it starts with, one song going on
and the other repeating.

Summer House

after Yannis Ritsos

We climbed the hill so we could see
our borrowed fields, the hills holding back
the sea, flanks of drying wheat. Hawks
and airplanes edged the sky. A lizard climbed the roses,
bees stitched the lavender. How did we soothe
each other with such carved hearts?
You disappeared into the woods, saving
the view for your camera. I followed
down the hill, and started dinner. Each morning
the fog lent us our wooden steps, our bicycles.
We earned the hills back by remembering their names.
Our nights ate away at the sea.

Big Boat

The day we discovered clammers crouching on the beach
with clam guns and canes and onion sacks,
wearing shorts in the cold rain, was also the day
we saw the boat. The clammers stared into the sand
like painters, open-legged, a gate the sandpipers ignored.
I'd been watching these pipers, hundreds of them,
cloud and sphere and turn, the top of their head
opening into a long blanket, then tightening
into a rolling ball over the tide, a sudden rest
as each would fall onto a waiting reed,
silence, then another rise, another turn.
Sometimes they would turn like colored paper,
one side white and the other dark, the page
flipping back and forth as though they were sure
something had been written there. We walked
towards the dunes, bottles of beer
foaming in our pockets, the wind
making scalps of everything. Climbing
in the threaded light we saw a small stone house
tucked between sand and forest.
A man on a ladder washed an upstairs window.
Behind the house a white mast
twice as high as the house tilted a little
until a red hill became its boat. It was in the water,
only there was no water. What is a canal but hope?
This giant absence a hundred pipers diving as one,
a hundred clams sinking fast, a hundred hands
planting themselves like trees in the sand,
root and root.

Middle Room

The middle room keeps all receipts, all plans.
The other rooms slope out forgivingly, more window than wall,
gray sea braced by a lone cedar more absently black
than the stone bowl on the living room floor.
More absently black,
a notion more lovely to the girl
the more it rains, as it does in sheets today,
neighbors vanished along with their plots
of bluebells and wagon wheels left to soften,
left by pioneers who'd found
the Pacific edged so tight, the view blocked
by such thick woods that the burning
took a whole summer
staring into the knuckled flames, the hissed
release of knots preserved in salt
drawing the peninsula's breath in around it.
Finally the smell of brightness covered this last mile,
though when they were through
the pioneers found new terrors: solo
on this mile-wide slip of sand, stumped,
new cabins' slur against the whittled bank: for safety
their daughters' daughters kept to the middle rooms,
little compromises hidden from sight,
safe under the coats of a few remaining cedars,
the girls' inner days a blanket
around the channeled oyster blade,
a defense around which even the newer houses are built
and stand bright and alone in each hard rain.
They built theirs together, just the two,
mouths full of nails to brace the beams. And now
you can hear their daughter shuffling cards,

she who's learning to play Memory,
returning through trial and error each snail
to its marbled shell, each kitten to its cat.
Nothing can pull her from her God-pairs.
It rains and she drags the child
back to its mother, sets them aside.

The Forest of Sure Things

In this land the children tear their hearts in half.
Let me explain. If ten things are wanted, only ten
can be had. If a stand of birches is found to be made of tin,
the soil around them will bleed with rust. In this land children
study their magazines in broad daylight, and in their books
any soldier who stumbles will not fall. No one will fall,
a gift parents try not to make much of. At every meal
some is set aside. In every garden a patch lies fallow. At parties
there are whispers of illegal cheeses. Camembert, especially,
is said to taste *alive*. And so the children learn
to make room. To leave some.
Nothing will come, but nothing will go.
To love like this half must rattle in its pit.

Dream at 39 Weeks

The green tooth of a river, sideways,
unturning, mechanical fish strung across the narrow mouth:

an old quarry in the middle of our city, as deep
as the buildings were tall. It hid

in the basement of the bank until a stuntman showed up,
yellow suit, rent-a-fence around the socket: we gathered

on the steep shore and he called us into the water. The fish
were real, waiting for coins. The quarry held, among other things,

other ways we could have gone. Softened boats
and our parents' clothes, everything we'd been afraid to want.

A dictionary of smells. The kitchen of the year she'd left, scrub pines,
sassafrass from the schoolyard and mossy tennis courts.

The stuntman brought a net, a purse net, gauze for the socket. We leaned in.
The fish rolled on their spindles. You and your typewriter ribbon,

you and your ship in a bottle, you and your fingering hands—
outside us I could hear the fish, the green fables they wound like clocks.

Still Life as Landscape

One September the seashore near town quit its ebb and flow.
It stayed. Who has stopped it, a woman asked, her ankles

unsinking, sand mute beneath her. There was no other sound
save the birds. The gulls dove easy in this new lake.

It was days before these fish learned what lake fish know:
there are only four sides, shadows are always trouble.

Without waves, without a start to stop at, you couldn't take
anything back. We hoped it was a glitch,

a toe in the drain or a typo in the almanac.
We ran pool vacuums and metal detectors over the sea floor,

hoping to budge what stuck. It was hard to turn in such sureness.
We rocked back on our heels, modeling a retreat.

The mayor declared it remarkable, this swelling stillness beneath us.
At the multiplex on Route 40, a documentary on beavers, what they do

to a place. Second only to man, the voice told us, as four hundred
aspen tottered into the lake, leaves rattling up like tossed coins.

The beavers do not mind the work. They have made a little room
for winter, a cabin above the ice where they wait like fishermen

for each other. We watched their year go by in the darkened theater.
Outside our sea held its breath.

Wake

The casseroles just showed up.
According to her sister a symbolic casting

of the feminine, not gender but *physics*, dear—
according to a friend she looked

just like her sister, green bathrobe mid-afternoon,
suitcase still in the trunk.

She'd carried him dead for days.
Out above the reeds a sphere of birds

stretches and knots, rises as one
brown then belly-white. Oh the hunger

when it came filled every chair.

Night Sailing

And so the ferns unleashed us.
I wanted to say this is it, this is our home
but they waved to us like strangers.
This is no land for planting—each old leaf
scrawls out a will, strawberry vines
root themselves from neck and tongue,
there are agreements we can't hear.
Still the sun is everywhere,
reeds seem to bow to us—
yesterday you were glad
to hear of a new bakery in town
finally a place we've never been.

***

The postmaster's husband
has given the week to an old maple,
some disease we can't see
but one he says is spreading; we won't know
until spring what else
to take down—their seven cats
weave curses round the fallen limbs
as he climbs down
from each new end,
each bare knuckle of tree.
To hesitate now is to let the worst in.

***

Even to say it.
Our ground, our yard

with its yellow fence:
in the company of night we carried him out
we said good words over his body
we said good words behind our fence
the space we'd left for zinnias
now our son
our son zinnia, our son elm.

On Forgetting

Your daughter has been waiting an hour.

You say you only have two hands, and she says
a stitch in time saves nine. She's learning

proverbs in school. She portends like an old woman.
You can barely speak to her. The sun reddens

your hands, your eyes. She wants Chinese tonight.
You turn the radio on loud. You can lead a horse to water,

or you can go jump in a lake. Go die, she says to you,
kicking the seat. You can't think how to stop her.

At a light, you recline your seat hard into little knees.
She needs to listen. Your own father was a man

among men, a force to be reckoned with.
You get on the beltway and watch a cycle lane-split.

A mile past your house is the lake where you fished
as a boy. Water, water everywhere, and say you've had a few.

Say this lake has some fine rainbow trout. Rod in the trunk,
no one back home. It's past dinnertime

and she won't look at you. Isn't a proverb just words
to keep you talking? That night let's say

you catch a shitload of fish. Fish out of water,
red fish, blue fish. The kid is finding you worms.

Let's say the sun sets, the fish rise, and you know
every constellation in the sky. You say *Cassiopeia, Little Bear*

and you get lucky, the stars are what she remembers.

Contingency Museum

The forgotten works wait in the underground vault

like cicadas. When there were footsteps above,
each brushstroke shone with hope,
canvas taut. But now the metal cabinets
holding these marginal works

have rusted a little, and taste
to the caretaker's daughter like monkey bars.

The smell of fresh paint frightens them both.
At the annual picnic, the caretaker
gave a speech on leaving things lay
that moved the collectors to tears.

The paintings wait like oxen.

Some winters the re-bar contracts,
raging sea stuck to a still life
of oranges and feather. The halls of the vault
were not built to support human weight.

Leave us, the girl cries out
but the paintings lean in,
press their thick skins to the glass.

Season

The oranges were the first to arrive,
bobbing along the coast like subtitles.
Everything seemed to carry another name.
Look at me, our mother said. Our lunch
a sacrifice, our hair a knotted map.
The youngest of us watched
his orange peel float out on the lake. The oldest
kept a tally of every shadow
creeping from barn to tree. Each seam,
each bud called out. From the earth
or the sea the next saint would rise.
The middle child carried with her
a scrap of wallpaper from the old dollhouse
and held it up against the shifting sky.

Dream House

Across the field a house
to which they had purposely left raw
the way. Only wings
or a path he'd mown
into the wheat, antlered bud
lit as it waited, down
whistling this and that shut.
She pushed dinner through,
bean soup, boated husks
reflected above his head: he turns
and what the field has learned
is let go, sung up
over the insulation,
this taking each other apart.

Horses

Forgive us our helplessness. Forgive us our horses.
Forgive us looking back for a flash of light
tunneling its way home, forgive us our flinching
as we reach towards clams held open. Forgive us the sound
of our digging. Forgive us our talk of marriage
as the old men bear down into the sand, fingers blue

and lonesome. Nothing in this blue
aches like they must, these men solitary horses
in an open field, withdrawing from their marriages
like clams in the dark, the whale eye of their wives' flashlights
beaming down. The boats their hearts sound
in heavy water: lurch, flinch.

For three days clams climb these numb hands, flinch
into the day, swell thick-tongued. Out of the blue
and into onion bags on each man's hip, a clicking sound
as they open to each other, stunning as the cock of a horse
reaching blind into the salty, stinging light.
Let our son go unnamed, let him have this marriage.

Not his hollow we flinch from, not marriage.
This path swallowed under the new sound.

Revision

After she left he made a habit
of her black windows, her dim lilacs.
Jade knives clattered on the fig tree.
He watched her house as though he

was watched, stumbling, trying to keep
his pace. He traced her from the extras
of his dreams, dinners, pacings.
His big work, a map of the inside of the earth,

grew dark with erasure. Facing the day,
his thin ships hesitated
to declare their sea, to follow
the dark gray current.

He took the children to the wide shore
where oranges were washing up two by two,
the herons occasionally lifting a knee,
winter and the ships farther out,

open-handed trees, open holds, explaining
how one knot undoes its brother,
his daughter counting the frozen oranges,
is this ours or are we waiting—

and later, the silvery hive, the front-page wreck.

Easement

She lets them tour her flagstone heart only after
the seas pull back, not on the days when eels
leer from her windows and the car earns its fishy smell.
Those days she's on the roof waving to helicopters.
Her hands shine once the Red Cross has gone,
after the dog has been found in the pear tree

                                        safe or not safe
and even after bulk trash day when everything she owned
lifts to reveal a wormy mess near the curb. Shining

above all else. Her family will move to an apartment,
settle on the top floor and never own carpet again.
She'll argue with her husband about insurance,
about lightning and if she takes the Holy Bible as evidence
for his blindness so help me God

                                 that is all right. Say it all.
Do they think this is who you are? Nights, you wait
on the balcony, hands on the railing and no one out there.
Wait until summer when the kids play Marco Polo
in the ocean, wait until your husband quits drinking.
Then what was not enough will be plenty
but again that will not be enough. Do not lean,
nothing will be solid. Carry his bottles out
to the balcony, to the fig tree with its braided trunk
and pour hard, leave the empties shining on the rail.

Green and brown reflections square you. Record
every meal, every step. Let the kitchen table rock
beneath casseroles: the man you love is home
every night. You burn dinner just to hear him
call your name. Twice you catch him casting ice cubes
like dice into the sink.

                          The freezer hums eternally.

You'll need this when he reads *Hints from Heloise*
before bed: ice tray a planter for seedlings, a pill sorter!
For rainy days, fill the garage with milk jugs, hide toothpicks
under the bed. Touch like fish near the surface of a pond,
not like water rushing over roots. Summer is over.
You must love him with a swallow of water under your tongue.
Our bodies are made of one-way doors that swing
and swing, always a crowd, pushing from what's happening
to what's not. See how long you can hold the door.
Fingerprints and ink will stick to your hands.

                                            Lift them.
You think it's not so much that Jesus walked on water
as that things wash up. So you've lost track of time—
your Christmas letter is an epic mess of fruit trees,
mobiles and saved furniture. That's fine.

                                    Water is nothing
without what stops it. Still, you're not sure what repeats,
when to leave a room. You stay too long at potlucks
not because of the changed years but because of the room
you've made for water in your life, the space you've left
for the tide. What we think of
as land is only
                  an inhalation, a shadow
of *not now*. Given this, it is clear what you must do:
turn your back on the ocean and climb your now-familiar stairs.
Imagine the giant squid roaming the dark depths, imagine it

waving from your window, yes, but also imagine the man
in bed beside you, your children and the stories they make up
about what happened to them when they were small.
The neighbor's cat creeps onto the balcony, upsetting
the bottles balanced there. A man in the street
looks up and sees them fall. Imagine his surprise,
silence gleaming down like a comet.

Two

Church

Our church was all brick, no name on it
and no stained glass. Every few years
a new preacher took over and tried to make us sing.
One told us Wile E. Coyote's lifelong quest
for the Road Runner was like us hungering for Jesus.
He said we all know Coyote never gets
the Road Runner. We said that's right. But no.
No, my friends: one time, Coyote
gets exactly what he prayed for. That skippety
Road Runner gets fat on radioactive birdseed
and this seed is the seed of Godliness, our Road Runner
big as a skyscraper. And Wile E. Coyote's dedication,
his constant prayers for this one thing, his need
to hold the baby Jesus in his own hands,
to not have to take it on faith—he gets what he wants.
That's right. Wile E. Coyote catches up
with the Road Runner, who's now a thousand times
his size. He grabs hold of the Road Runner's leg
with his tiny little hand. He's caught him.
Coyote never thought this would happen. He's built
his whole life around this one goal. Put himself
out of work is what he's done, my friends.
Our Coyote holds up a little sign
saying "now what?" We waited.
Then one Sunday the preacher's gone, a stranger
in his place, wearing his robes. The fan
on high, lilies asea. One of you, he shouts, is free.
One of you will not have to pay the piper.
One of you will walk this earth and you shall not
stumble and you shall not thirst. One of you
is lost and you shall not be found. We left,

each one of us. Some did come back. Some
only went as far as the laundry line before missing
the feel of slippers on carpet. Some watched the sky
that night and took comfort in the blinking radio tower.
Some flew. There was so much to be undone.

Tether

Nothing is ever the same as they said it was.
It's what I've never seen before that I recognize.

—DIANE ARBUS

Recording

The first person in recorded history
struck by a comet slept on her couch
across the road from the Comet Drive-In

and the comet found her roof, her sadness, her knee,
and woke her. Everything that hurts

hurt before, she said. Showing at the drive-in, a documentary
on tightrope-walking: a young man frustrated
that his dream, the World Trade Center, was not yet built

so he practiced for years in a meadow crossing intended sky, intent
like a pillowcase sweetening him, no harm … Here

let the towers go, let them write him crossing, cursive, back and forth

his name steadying our tongues … Famous, overcoat
floating down without him, the idea that we stand

where we mean to stand, 1974, a distraction

from my parents' morning commute. At 59th Street they split.
The poems I was writing were no longer poems of their divorce,

my father's sweeping gestures or his pain, the old Volkswagen
and garden hose—all of that had washed from my poems

and instead an imaginary family arrived in borrowed gardens,
their son stillborn—even as I grew heavy with my own son
I wrote poem after poem holding this imagined horror close.

Exhibit at the L.A. Central Library: Acrostic at 7 Weeks

Writers and Their Reasons, a last-minute display
Halfway up the escalator, replacing *Abandoned*
Early Careers of the Masters. Stung roots,
Razor clams, the mess clammers make of the shore.
Each proud meal. Maurice Sendak
Told of the strangers who descended,
Hungarian, his aunts and uncles
Expanding into the hall, all reach,
Wanting his cheeks, the food
In his mouth, the stale corners of his attention.
Lines crosshatched where stiff monsters bent,
Drew back. Shadowing them: overexposed photos,
The writers squinting from someone's backyard,
Hostas behind them, gin
In hand, Mother dead by now. A month
No one was much interested in but me.
Given reason, given lunch, I wore a rut,
Staring into their sprung mouths.
Afterwards I'd walk back to the office,
Ruining a poem buried under Outlook, under Word,
Earliest version of your body fastening inside me.

Seven Year Acrostic

Applecart, I signed my letters, and help,
Love, Dana. That wasn't my name. None were.
Every year I tried to O the
X. Syllables fell on me like pelts
And soon I was the gewurtztramminer
No one orders in restaurants. Enough
Dear. Henry buries matchsticks for practice,
Eulogizes their not-fires, not-help, not-
Redburning beds. In Harlem I watched
A rooster panic in a traffic circle,
Not a hazard yet, not yet. I was
Doing my job, an inspector for the City,
Terrified of the empty page.
Hours later he was still alive, safe from my report.
Eventually I left him there, unrecorded,
To find my way home: borrowed sofa,
Endive, unreachable green in the lot behind me.
Renters, all of us, in our inward-facing
Rooms where we waited for the view to open up.
I papered the walls with poems,
Bills, applications, all of them
Late. Here is the X of that year, mistakes
Everywhere let live; here is my record.
How I painted shut the windows, curtained
Over my anger. What
Rooster? I could have stayed there,
Radio-fed and off the clock, barely there.
Ira upstairs in Maps, forgive me.
Barely where. Today the postmaster asks for my best
Letterman story and I give him the rooster.
Everyone in line behind me, sorry about that.
Noon and my actual days get lost in plot. What's the purpose
Of God, Henry asks his dying matchsticks.

God will letter your red days, read your letters
O redheaded dead. The matchyard spreads
Out towards the neighbor's peonies, family
Dinner on the patio not-burning. They wave.
Virgin wood, there's the wreck you could become,
Eating through the curtains, the manicured lawn.
Rest please, says Henry. Under this earth all
Your talking goes. All your these and those.
Bed by bed he tucks the whalebones in
And washes them with a hose.
Don't you think they might want up?
Down, says Henry, down God.
All right. Here's a rock for their heads.
You bury their names in what you said.

Parks Inspector

What the land did wrong I wrote down
and it was fixed. That winter I read the Russians

in my government car, waiting for branches to break
high above the sidewalk. My reports

foretold all possible pain:
heart sunk on a stump, fingers

hinge-sheared, bitten curb.
A cold-patch truck followed me

and wardens hid in their huts. I went home
to a borrowed dog I dragged through the snow,

a favor for the traveling writer whose ferns I let thicken
like fingernails, his similes in pairs unused on the wall.

Sunday Nights at 8/7 Central

Recorded, our lives run forward
and so I carry this fear of sudden words:
as a girl I'd type telegrams on the keyboard

of our dark computer to let aliens know I was no threat,
here's where I am, this house, this room, this highway:
stop I would say to avoid pressing enter—that silent machine

let me keep typing while my father mowed the lawn, his young head
marking our place from the sky, my words melting
into song, into dust, all of it I know I'll never need, I'll never use up,

my useless words: hello stop today I wore my blue shirt stop imagine:
my telegrams safe with the aliens, no film
to show us ugly as we were, no one

to do a thing. The uselessness of murder clues, standing water
a melted icicle, constellations above a body
marking the spray of blood on a headboard,

this useless river
of solutions, this burr
in my heart, these backspaced calls.

Cynghanedd for Route 40

This morning I've stayed in sight, your man
in the fields, doubling back: a fanbelt again, Dad, a leash.

Our triple bypass, our rebuilt A&P,
graveyard, idea, gasoline: we argued every day, slowing

to let in West Baltimore, air. Our battle lost to me now,
bypassed. Old sycamores a simple bedside, cars

a dialtone against the sheet. Nothing to steal. A day
of doughnuts and arabbers, beauty of hand and sugar

on Lexington Avenue, vixen leaning out,
or the three good ballgames I all but read through.

Tell me again about the drive that began late, lime
from the holiday party desiccating on the dash, Diane merges out
        perfectly

and by sunrise you make it there: Ocean City, dinky but you see
        cormorants, each one
unfolding like those years behind you, here flung out by a knot
        loosed

in darkness, the drive home to us hard, nervous, kind.

Superstition

We couldn't see the picture until after it was painted,
or the mirror until our hair had frozen. We couldn't walk
after dark, the graves so close together, who knew
how their legs lay, what word lay on the tips of their tongues.

Years ago in the blue house on Laurel Hill Lane,
the young girl couldn't breathe right. We caught a trout,
alive and gasping, and we held its head in her mouth,
the two of them desperate in their eyes. When we let the trout go

we knew it had swallowed some of the girl's pain
because it surfaced so often, coughing. There are two ways
to keep track of what happened: at night, if you turn the air
to stone you will know what moves. In daylight,

wear hands where your hands would be, breathe
what leaves you. Whatever you do
turns, the omens pin you to your table, your favorite chair:
at last someone has named each vine, each mouth, each trout.

After Zoe's Baptism

We were not ourselves in the car,
my sister safe in her carseat, holy water
drying in the creases of her legs,
our parents stiff in their suits.
Everyone waiting for us at the hotel,
my sister the only one of us saved.
Curried lamb, baklava, little gold-rimmed cups
surround her Christ table,
her Christ bib, gifts lifting the tables.
Out in the lobby a boy holds a call
of surprise in his throat, works it around.
Another band sets up in the corner.
The boy hides his hands,
counts who among us
he'd save from a burning building,
what he'd make us leave.

Music of Plants

The plants grew and grew,
whispering as they inched back from the radio.

They swung on plastic hangers, neck
and neck, the lucky one fed cantatas an hour a day.

Of course the cat ate some. Our suppers
were quick, no frying, windows green

and gridded above our anger. My houseplants
kept calling, birthless, as my mother

carried boxes down the hall,
my three plants taking

the music into their leaves, drum-stunted
or waltzed into bloom. Forgotten days

I recorded later, once we knew which survived.

The Calling

So gentle with nouns his fingers shook,
the young typesetter kept to his side of the bed.

The phone would ring. It rang all night
with requests for tomorrow's word, tomorrow's quote.

Had it always been like this? Spring in its haste
swelled his front door but still callers fit love letters beneath it.

You are the only one who knows, they began, and I am afraid
to tell anyone but I have sinned. My father was a monster.

I ran the dog into a snow bank. I did not leave a deposit
and have covered my scuff marks with furniture.

I filled creamer with sugar. I left him calling my name in the yard.
I said you may not sit with me at lunch. You may not call.

The typesetter kept a room for this, and he let the letters rise into hills.
When it was time to make a new word he reached for the bottom
            layer of paper,

the richest, and when he paused, it shook. Bees flew from the sorrow
and when they died, lighter than air, he strung their bodies into sound.

Chincoteague Island

It was Blue and Red and a nice county fair. On the Ferris Wheel, fast and small, Blue and Red. "Hit Me Baby One More Time" ran through their skins and off in the dark the ponies nodded to each other. In the same dark the men had chosen this year's ponies, whispering then shouting. A few long hairs washed up. Blue and Red had not seen the ponies swim, but they'd heard their new names in the air. Blue turned to Red in the swinging chair. Blue took Red's hand, and the bus on the gravel was silent. They didn't see the cherry of the driver's cigarette. It was not their bus. The night held them up like chalk to a chalkboard.

Honeymoon

Aguas Calientes

Our first night we ate with a crowd of Germans
fresh from the ruins. They toasted their luck,
their wives, the miraculous cheese.
Potatoes and trout appeared before us,
ears of corn with lobes the size of dimes.
This town with its wheelbarrows
and steam baths was changing its name
to that of the next town,
now abandoned. We walked the one road
back to our hotel, steam rising from us
into the blank slate of trees.

Machu Picchu

Through the ruins' turnstile
miles of stairs, no landings,
this and that room cut into the face
and the face turned from us.
You were talking about Oysterville, the flat spit
of our future, our children
with their heavy bare heads
waiting on some far shore. All day
we walked these halls, naming them,
as the town filled with other mayors,
other newlyweds. Here they laid out their dead
and here they washed their hands.
Our children, you said,
will forget we were here.

Confession

I used to pretend the ceiling was the floor.
Room for everything, window seats
on roof beams, corners and corners
of untouched chairs. I haven't told you
how I loved the Spiegel catalog—husband
in new robe, wife on banded ottoman—or how
I faked my way through office job
after job, the boss's approach triggering
my blind clamor on the keyboard,
gamble of letters the sound of quick work.
(His retreat, my hand on the backspace.)
All this backpedaling and you wonder
what was really there. Ottoman
ottoman. The beauty of an unwalked floor.

As Light As Dark

Last night as we left the museum
there were no lights, just pale roses
bordering the path out.
There is a word for this
but I can't remember it, a word
for the sky in balance, just as light
as dark. For years I have tried to call it up.
I long for it most when I'm someplace new,
strange lawn furniture darkening into sky
as roses whiten, shadows unhook
from table and post. Lately
I can't seem to hold a single thing—
my keys are gone, hair scripts the sink,
even the good days seem rolled
in some other carpet.
May this slipping away protect us,
may the loss of days ease the ones I love
from their anger, that sturdy chair
circled all day by its shadow, without which
a dim sea would come to level our yard, level
as in make right.

41 Weeks

One of the stories I told had happened.
Like how the town itself was once covered in vines.

The other had not happened yet—that night
we played Carcassone across the ballast of my body,

a city-building game in which fields are taken
by whoever most wants them: whose soldiers

lay down at noon in the fields, dreaming
as they guess the wheat's length, its shorn weight …

Our friend kept winning, my husband and I reduced
to quarrels over walls, bridges, the baby

knuckling my ribs, kicking off my dark wall—or
not, no, you slept in the field and would not wake.

We said our goodnights. We rode
rootbound to the hospital and waited.

The room filled. My odd stillbirth poems
elbowed the machines, their skittery graph of your whale-heart

far offshore. The borrowed story keeping time.
The surgeon cut a quick, crooked line

and lifted you then from the dream of blue walls,
lifted you crying and safe, unwritten.

Narrative Distance

In two days the rat swam 400 meters
to the other island, also empty, in search
of another rat. The scientists
who had been following the rat
grew desperate as the weeks passed
and the peanut butter went stale.
No song from the radio collar.
Their wives wanted a vacation.
It was summer, the bee-bitten lilacs
turned in, some as-yet-unnamed tree
parted a soft slab of rock. They sent another rat out.
And another.

November

Daily they circled the lake.
The new birds wore a white stripe,
pale against the unsealed lake.
They sank and sank, these birds,
they fell from the sky. And shook it off.
They gripped each other
in the water like Italian tourists. If one day
was unlike another
the water did not show it.
The mother could say, here, these leaves are burning
and the son would not look round.
       So she did not say it.

       Someone—boys—
had thrown old jack o'lanterns in the lake
so everyone could watch their faces
soften and nod.
These days so new.

Living Room Acrostic

The snake and the caterpillar are both very hungry.
Henry drags them under the table,
Eats the page where Minnie hides the cake knife.
Verily it was taped to the dish. She fished her wish.
Every day I hear him pulling bodies from the shelf:
Roar, says Henry, book book book.
Years ago, I say, there were three snakes and one
Hoped the others would fall asleep so she could write a poem
Using their hunger to fill the page. No.
Now the snake has eaten everyone we know.
Grandma, God, the goats you barely saw
Running through the clover of page eight
Year after year. You want to save them,
Call back the tunneling to its egg, its goat heart.
All you have wanted and yet you Google.
The punched holes fit Henry's snaking fingers. He wears where it was.
Eat me, sings the snake into the latched goat-field.
Rock me. Forget the metaphor you were saving for later.
Put it out to pasture and if it returns
I'll hold open the page of its joy,
Lick shut its open heart. Undrawn
Lamb of the living room, alphabet
Arlene Sardine forgot: your hunger
Rabbiting from ark to unplowed field.

Cynghanedd

Kids' consignment stores: dust on smocks, nitrogen,
the dollar rack, or really, death.
An edible costume on sale. *CDB,*
paperback his mother hated. A customer: *huh, okay, bye.* Pipe.
What the living outgrow, gently. The wet hive
gummed with decoration, a damaged cow, mother
dreaming *panna cotta* over a dragon mitten, pincer
unpurled across the aisle. Under the sea or scalp
only flight, monuments. Age. Flannel to hem.
Other years the old chrysanthemum man came
in to say hi. Even the heaviest vanish, youth on TV
adjusting their loss like scarves: last Darjeeling, skis, Christ.

At the Visionary Art Museum

The first brother's boat could hold no water, his toothpicks neither pressure-treated nor waxed. He had to keep a fan running to stave off the mint. Across town, the boat maker's twin brother began to plot his own escape. His boat would be in a bottle, the traditional style, and just might float. Their father, like many gods, was a river and the brothers shared a hankering for salt. They waited until nightfall, they waited for the spring clearance sale at Joe Daniel's Restaurant Supply Store. It was a secret that weighed an ounce. One brother helped the other, thousands of tiny logs cupped by hand to make room for the tiny crew's sleeping quarters below deck. One pulled the cord and tissue sails tore at their staples. No matter. The river rolled on, hungry for the fish it held. The twins would need new bottles, more glue. These boats take years. These boats break under the weight of the dust of the years it takes to build them.